GALAXY OF SUPERSTARS

Ben Affleck

Backstreet Boys

Garth Brooks

Mariah Carey

Cameron Diaz

Leonardo DiCaprio

Tom Hanks

Hanson

Jennifer Love Hewitt

Lauryn Hill

Ewan McGregor

Mike Myers

'N Sync

LeAnn Rimes

Britney Spears

Spice Girls

Jonathan Taylor Thomas

Venus Williams

CHELSEA HOUSE PUBLISHERS

GALAXY OF SUPERSTARS

Tom Hanks

Jim McAvoy

CHELSEA HOUSE PUBLISHERS
Philadelphia

Frontis: *Tom Hanks's shy smile and modest manner project the image of the
ordinary guy next door, even when winning his second Oscar.*

Produced by
21st Century Publishing and Communications, Inc.
New York, New York
http://www.21cpc.com

CHELSEA HOUSE PUBLISHERS

Editor in Chief: Stephen Reginald
Managing Editor: James D. Gallagher
Production Manager: Pamela Loos
Art Director: Sara Davis
Director of Photography: Judy L. Hasday
Senior Production Editor: LeeAnne Gelletly
Publishing Coordinator: James McAvoy
Cover Designer: Terry Mallon

Front Cover Photo: Jez/London Features Int'l
Back Cover Photo: Photofest

The Chelsea House World Wide Web address is
http://www.chelseahouse.com

3 5 7 9 8 6 4 2

Library of Congress Cataloging-in-Publication Data

McAvoy, Jim.
  Tom Hanks / by Jim McAvoy.
  64 p. cm. – (Galaxy of superstars)
  Filmography: p. 61
  Includes bibliographical references and index.
  Summary: A biography of the actor who won two consecutive Academy
Awards for his roles in the films "Philadelphia" and "Forrest Gump."
  ISBN 0-7910-5235-4 (hc.) — ISBN 0-7910-5335-0 (pb.)
  1. Hanks, Tom—Juvenile literature 2. Motion picture actors and actresses—
United States—Biography—Juvenile literature. [1. Hanks, Tom. 2. Actors and
actresses.] I. Title. II. Series.
PN2287.H18M39   1999
791.43'028'092—dc21
[B]   99—32042
                                                                              CIP
                                                                              AC

Dedication: *For the true friends in my life. You know who you are.*

CONTENTS

1

PHENOMENON

In 1993, just before the release of the eagerly awaited drama *Philadelphia*, movie star Tom Hanks was interviewed by *The Philadelphia Inquirer.* Although the Jonathan Demme AIDS film had not yet premiered, Tom already had one hit movie that year, *Sleepless in Seattle.* He was about to add another to his credits.

In the interview Hanks discussed his most successful previous year, 1988, when the film *Big* made Tom Hanks a huge star. He called that year "a fluke," commenting, "A year like 1988 comes once every 15 years if you're lucky, once every 10 years if you're amazingly lucky, and once every five if you're a phenomenon." Tom repeated this same sentiment to several other news sources, not knowing that he was, in fact, describing his acting career, both past and future.

Fast forward to early on February 9, 1999, when actor Kevin Spacey and an officer from the Academy of Motion Picture Arts and Sciences announced the nominees for the 71st Academy Awards in Beverly Hills. One of the front runners, with 11 nominations, including Best Picture,

Already laden with a host of awards honoring his phenomenal rise to stardom, Tom enjoys another honor reserved for Hollywood's royalty. With wife Rita Wilson, he leaves his handprints in the cement in front of Mann's Chinese Theater in Los Angeles.

Best Director, and Best Original Screenplay, was the war drama *Saving Private Ryan*. Tom Hanks, the film's star, was also nominated as Best Actor. It was the fourth nomination of his career, and if he won, it would be his third Oscar victory in only six years.

The nomination was not a surprise. Those who had seen Steven Spielberg's World War II epic when it premiered in July 1998 knew the ambitious, unforgettable film and its lead actor were assured of Academy Award nominations and a slew of other awards. Its 30-minute opening sequence, recreating the Normandy invasion of 1944, was a small masterpiece itself. Many of the most influential film critics repeatedly hailed *Saving Private Ryan* as one of the best films of the year.

The film's outstanding success was just a small taste of things to come for Hanks in the extremely successful period that started in 1998. In December of that year, the prolific Hanks was on-screen again. In *You've Got Mail* he appeared in the familiar guise of romantic leading man with costar Meg Ryan. He also made the rounds of the television award shows for the HBO miniseries he produced, *From the Earth to the Moon,* the largest original HBO production ever undertaken. It won three Emmy Awards, including Outstanding Mini-series, as well as the Golden Globe Award in the same category.

Although Tom did not win a third Oscar for *Saving Private Ryan*, he did receive other notable distinctions. He was nominated for a Screen Actors Guild Award, a People's Choice Award (which he won), and a Golden Globe Award. In March of 1999 he was named ShoWest Star of the Decade at the ShoWest

Convention in Las Vegas. ShoWest is the annual conference of the National Association of Theatre Owners, where highly anticipated summer films are previewed. The theater owners bestow honors on the stars who have had the biggest impact on movies and profits. The theater owners' pick of Tom Hanks as star of the decade confirmed what many people already knew: this guy, who from 1988 to 1998 had helped his films take in more than $1.3 billion in ticket sales, was here to stay.

Tom Hanks is not the kind of actor to boast about such formidable accomplishments.

In the film Big, *Tom won accolades for his charming portrayal of a 13-year-old boy in a man's body who, among other feats, danced across a giant keyboard. His performance won him his first Academy Award nomination.*

Tom's incredibly successful 1998 began with the release of Saving Private Ryan, *in which he took on one of his most dramatic roles. In the opening sequence of the film, Hanks (at right) and his men approach the beaches at Normandy.*

However, he is often compared to the late screen legend James Stewart or to revered actor Jack Lemmon, two other male stars equally adept at both drama and comedy. Hanks is perceived as the all-American "regular guy" who touches us with his poignant performances in films of all genres. It doesn't matter if he falls in love with a mermaid (*Splash*), heroically fights both discrimination and a deadly disease (*Philadelphia*), happens into some of recent history's most memorable events (*Forrest Gump*), or conducts a romance over the Internet (*You've Got Mail*). Whatever his character is doing, audiences can't help but watch—and care about him. As *Biography* magazine has written: "To men, he's a guy's guy who always comes through in a pinch. To women, he's the guy next door, the one your mother always wanted you to date, and the one you hope you'll end up with."

To be so accepted by your audience and to have the respect and admiration of your peers is something of which every actor dreams. For Tom Hanks, it's reality. He is, by his own description, that very rare Hollywood creature: a true, enduring phenomenon. But he did not become one overnight.

2

BEGINNINGS

The actor that most reminds audiences of the "guy next door" did not in fact have a traditional family upbringing. Close friend and two-time costar Sally Field told *People* magazine that "he comes from a non-family. He was a boy in search of a family."

Thomas J. Hanks was born on July 9, 1956, in Concord, California, to Amos and Janet Hanks. He joined older siblings Sandra, now a writer, and Larry, currently a college professor. Several years after Tom's birth, his younger brother, Jim, who also became an actor, made his debut in the family.

Tom's parents did not have a happy marriage, however, and they separated several times. One night Amos Hanks, a restaurant chef, packed up the three oldest children and moved to Reno, Nevada. Janet Hanks, a hospital employee and homemaker, kept custody of young Jim. When Tom's parents divorced, he was just five years old.

As a hotel chef, Amos Hanks moved from place to place with his children. He remarried twice, giving Tom at least half a dozen step-siblings at one time. Although

Tom became intrigued with acting as a teenager when he performed in high-school productions. He also discovered he was good at both comedy and drama, talents he would successfully display throughout his career.

the instability of life with Amos was at times hard on the young boy, Tom and the other kids eventually adapted and even embraced their unusual home life. Besides, Tom has said, the moves cured his eventual boredom with wherever they were living at the time.

All in all, Tom was a pretty normal kid, skinny with dark brown hair, who frequently fantasized about far-off places. He liked to memorize the names of space-shuttle crews and the stars in the sky, some of which he can still recite from memory. When he entered junior high school, his father had married a Chinese woman named Frances Wong, and the now very sizable family settled in Oakland, California. Tom has described the situation: "We're all pretty close now, but it was rough for a while. My dad's third wife, Frances, is a wonderful lady, but we made it very hard on her at first. We were awful. . . . I was only ten when she came along and I'd been living alone with my dad for a long time and it was like—no one's going to tell me what to do. It took a while to adjust."

Tom was not an exceptional student, but he did enjoy school and the audiencelike atmosphere that was developing around him. He learned to work a crowd using his natural charm to make friends with the other kids. "I liked being the new kid in the class. It was always two days of being shy, and then boom, you're in with the unit, and you get elected social chairman," he recalled.

At Skyline High School, Tom took part in athletics and also joined the local born-again Christian group for young people. Looking back on this period, Tom feels that spirituality grounded him. "It was one of the best things I ever did," he said in an interview. "I had been a

confused kid. Religion helped me."

Tom discovered something else at this time —acting. After watching a friend's performance in *Dracula,* he became interested in acting for himself, and took a part in his high-school production of the musical *South Pacific.* According to drama teacher Rawley Farnsworth, Tom stole the show as the comically scheming sailor Luther. In a change of pace, he followed that role with a performance in the Tennessee Williams dark drama *Night of the Iguana.*

Junior college was next for the novice actor. Tom was accepted for a two-year program at Chabot Junior College in Hayward, California,

Charming and exuberant, Tom has been a natural at making others laugh ever since he was a teenager. It is a talent he would later put to good use in his films, such as in this scene from one of his early comedy successes, Punchline.

and began taking classes in the fall of 1974. Enrolling in the Drama in Performance class, Tom assumed it was an acting course. In fact, it was a class in which students read plays and then went to see them locally performed. For Tom, taking the class was an important "mistake." He took in performance after performance in the theaters of San Francisco. Usually unable to convince his college friends to accompany him, Tom went alone, which turned out to be the best thing possible. As he recalled:

> I was just swept away, really shaken . . . impressed by how actors could get up on the stage and communicate from a blueprint a guy had made forty years before! Here it was, coming to life—you could almost reach out and touch it. I didn't so much decide to become an actor as I decided that working in the theater connected me to an amazing source of energy I wasn't going to find anywhere else. I wanted to be part of it!

Tom attended Eugene O'Neill's drama *The Iceman Cometh*, which was staged at the nearby Berkeley Repertory Theater. The performances and the production literally changed Tom's life. From then on, he felt he had a goal. Somehow, in some way, he was going to be a part of this thing called acting, whether it was as a crew member or the guy in charge of lighting. It didn't matter. He just had to be involved.

Winning a scholarship as a stage carpenter, Tom transferred to California State University at Sacramento in 1976. It was at Cal State that he began to seriously consider a career in acting. It was there that he also met a fellow student-actor, Susan Dillingham, who would soon begin using the professional name Samantha Lewes. Tom and Samantha found they had much in common and soon started dating.

Encouraged by Samantha, Tom auditioned for a production of Anton Chekhov's *The Cherry Orchard* being staged at the Sacramento Civic Theater. He won the part, and also found a good friend and mentor in Vincent Dowling, the director of the play. Dowling was also the artistic director of the Great Lakes Shakespeare Festival in Cleveland, Ohio, and he invited Tom and other cast members to take unpaid internships with the festival over the summer of 1977. Although the work would vary, there was a possibility that the interns would get small roles in some of the festival's productions.

Dowling was a Hanks fan from the very beginning: "When I came home that afternoon [after seeing Hanks act for the first time], I told my wife there was one kid who had star quality. I said, 'He's like a young Tony Curtis, but I think he has even more potential.'"

Life in Cleveland was an all-around theater experience for Tom. Aside from acting, he apprenticed unofficially in everything from stage lighting to building sets. During that first summer, Tom also decided to drop out of college. He stayed with the Shakespeare Festival for the next two years, acting in several plays and making a modest living.

In 1978, Tom received his first acting honor, the Cleveland Drama Critics Award for his performance as the evil Proteus in *The Two Gentlemen of Verona*. Although Tom was excited by his newfound success and continued playing in Shakespearean classics, he

Hoping that his stage experience would pay off on Broadway, Tom and his young family moved to New York City's Times Square area where he would be close to theaters. Although success on the New York stage eluded him, it was here that he got his first break in films.

wanted to give the bright lights of Broadway a try. Selling his car for expense money, he and Samantha relocated to New York City and settled into a small apartment. Here, their first child, a son named Colin, was born, and Tom and Samantha were married in a small church wedding.

While living in the Times Square area, in the heart of the theater district, the young actor actively sought an agent to represent him. He also joined the Riverside Shakespeare Company to gain acting experience. However, this position offered no salary, and the young couple's financial situation was rough. Sandra Hanks, Tom's sister, remembers returning empty soda containers so that she could send Tom and his new family a small sum of money. Tom did get an agent in New York, but in the summer of 1979 he returned to Cleveland where he could make some money acting at the Great Lakes Shakespeare Festival.

When he returned to New York City in the fall of 1979, Tom Hanks found that, while he was in Cleveland, his new agent had helped him land his first film role.

MAKING A SPLASH

The movie Tom's agent had gotten for him was a "slasher film"—a horror movie called *He Knows You're Alone.* The film follows a bride to be as she is stalked by a deranged killer who strikes on the eve of her wedding. Tom played the part of Elliot, a psychology student.

Tom's part was very small—(his screen time ran only about seven minutes)—and the movie was not very good (Tom later commented the film's budget was "about forty dollars"). However, *He Knows You're Alone* was important because it helped get Tom into the Screen Actors Guild, a union for people in the film industry. The $800 he earned also helped keep him and his family afloat for a while longer. And it led to his next role, the lead in a CBS TV movie titled *Mazes and Monsters.*

Taking a cue from early-1980s teenagers' near obsession with the role-playing game "Dungeons and Dragons," the 1982 film centers around a group of young outsiders who gather to play "Mazes and Monsters" in order to escape the troubles of their everyday lives. Tom flexed some early dramatic muscle in the film—at one point, his character

Tom and Peter Scolari were the stars of Bosom Buddies, *a sitcom about two guys who dress up as women in order to live cheaply in a women's hotel. The part might not have been quite what Tom was looking for, but it led to his making a splash in a film that would change the direction of his career.*

considers suicide—and because it was on television, he gained his greatest exposure to date.

This role got Tom several auditions with the ABC television network, trying out with dozens of other struggling actors for various roles in different series the network had planned for the 1980–81 season. One of those series was *Bosom Buddies*, a situation comedy produced by the same people responsible for the hit *Happy Days* and its spin-off, *Laverne & Shirley*.

The premise of the new show was simple: advertising executive friends Kip Wilson and Henry Desmond share a New York City apartment in a building that is about to be demolished, and they need a new place to live. Luckily, their friend Amy finds them a vacant apartment in her building. There is a catch, however. The Susan B. Anthony Hotel is a rooming house for females only; they will have to dress as women to live there. From then on, Kip and Henry assume the feminine identities of "Buffy" and "Hildegarde."

A couple of auditions later, Tom had been selected for the part of Kip/Buffy and Peter Scolari, also relatively unknown, was chosen to play Henry/Hildegarde. When asked why he picked Tom as one of the two leads, executive producer Chris Thompson replied simply, "He was funnier than anyone else." *Bosom Buddies* co-producer Ian Praiser heaped accolades on Tom, remarking, "The first day I saw him on the set, I thought, 'Too bad he won't be in television for long.' I knew he'd be a movie star in two years."

Bosom Buddies was picked up by ABC and premiered Thanksgiving night, November 27, 1980. Sandwiched between the popular comedies *Mork & Mindy* and *Barney Miller*, the first episode was the seventh most-watched program that week, an excellent rating for a new show.

Although the show continued to do well, it was not the success its first airing had predicted it would be. Tom and Peter were generally praised, however, for their chemistry together. In fact, the two did share a great partnership on the set, making up lines on the spot—ad-libbing—and becoming friends off the set.

During the show's run, Tom was making $9,000 an episode, his career was thriving, and he was having the time of his life. "We had a lot of fun doing the show, and the good time we were having came across on-screen. It was a major learning experience to me," he said. The only downside was having to frequently change into women's clothes, often in front of the studio audience.

In the series' second season, 1981–82, the guys reveal their secret to the rest of their pals, and the show then relied much less on the sight of its two male leads in drag and more on the crazy situations the two got themselves into: using a computer to date women, who turned out to be devil worshipers, or flashing back to their younger days while attending a high-school reunion.

Unfortunately, ABC moved the show to different time slots three times during the 1981–82 season, eventually dooming the series. After 38 episodes, two seasons, and by then worsening ratings, the sitcom was canceled. Even a campaign that netted 35,000 letters of protest from upset viewers couldn't save it.

After the cancellation of *Bosom Buddies*, Tom made the rounds of several other sitcoms, guest starring on *Taxi, Happy Days,*

and on NBC's *Family Ties* as the alcoholic
uncle of Michael J. Fox's character.

It was the guest spot on *Happy Days* that
would have the greatest impact on Tom's
future. On the set, he met Ron Howard, former
star of *Happy Days* and *The Andy Griffith
Show*. Since the late 1970s, Howard had
wanted to make the leap to big-time film
director and, in fact, had directed two films
and a few TV movies. In 1983, looking for
another film, he settled on a quirky comedy
about an average guy who falls for a mermaid.
Several well-known actors were either too
busy or not interested in playing main character Allen Bauer. So the script, titled *Splash*,
fell to Tom Hanks, whom Howard had remembered from *Happy Days*. "The word was real
good on Tom Hanks around town. He read [for
the role], and he was terrific. We just stopped
looking," said Howard.

Hanks thinks about it differently. "The only
reason I got that part was because absolutely
no one else would do it. . . . Ron Howard was so
desperate, he had to try his luck with me—a
complete novice who had no idea what he was
doing. Thank God."

Few could have predicted the film's impact
on its stars, director, and studio. Tom Hanks
was not by any means a household name, and
neither were Canadian John Candy, who
played Allen's playboy brother Freddie, nor
Daryl Hannah, who had made only a couple of
movies before she was cast as Madison the
mermaid.

Making the film was a risk. Ron Howard
had not yet proved himself as a "real" director.
In addition, a rival studio had a competing
project called *Mermaid*, which had attracted

25

MAKING   MAKING A SPLASH

*Sometimes called the
original nice guy, former
child actor Ron Howard
boosted Tom's career
when he gave him the
lead in the film* Splash.
*Howard had remem-
bered Tom from one of
the actor's guest spots
on a TV show, and the
two became friends as
well as collaborators.*

bigger names. But when a strike by the actors'
union kept that film from being made, *Splash*
was given a go by the Disney company's new
wing, Touchstone Pictures. Up to that time,
Disney had been known primarily for its animated films and comedies directed toward
children and families. This movie was geared
mainly toward adults, and it featured brief
mermaid nudity. It also got a PG (parental
guidance) rating. The film was exactly what
Disney needed to position Touchstone as its
more "adult" division.

Tom and costar Daryl Hannah share a kiss at the end of the film
Splash. Although the film featured relative unknowns such as
Hannah and John Candy, as well as the novice director Ron
Howard, it was a hit with audiences and critics alike.

Critics were generally positive, including the influential *New York Times*, which wrote, "*Splash* could have been shorter, but it probably couldn't have been much sweeter." Audiences loved the movie—and its attractive stars. Opening on March 9, 1984, it was the surprise hit of the year, eventually raking in more than $110 million at theaters and much more when it was later released on home video. Finally, Tom was in a hit movie.

"I didn't think it would be a stinker, maybe a little cartoonish, but the first weekend I get a call. 'Six million bucks at the box office.' You're in your first big film. It's beyond my comprehension. That's a lot of money. . . . It's perfect," Tom said later of *Splash*'s success.

Both the star and his director were happy with Hanks's transition to the big screen and the range of emotions he brought to the role. Not only was he funny but he also made the audience sympathize with him and care about what happened to him and his nautical girl-friend. Tom Hanks was on his way to being much more than a working, recognizable actor. He was about to become a star.

4

HITS AND MISSES

After the huge success of *Splash,* Hollywood began to realize that Tom Hanks might just be the next big male star in movies. Scripts soon flooded in, and Tom was kept busy. Even before the mermaid comedy was released, he was hard at work on his next film, the sex-comedy *Bachelor Party.* The film, about an over-the-top male ritual, was a sleeper hit in theaters and went on to do well on cable and as a video rental. It also helped to further establish Hanks as one of the new leading men of the 1980s.

Many critics panned *Bachelor Party* as just another "party movie" like *Porky's* or *Animal House,* but generally praised Tom's performance as the film's saving grace. He was also compared to comic actor Bill Murray more than once. Audiences, too, seemed to remember the guy who was so appealing in that mermaid movie. *Bachelor Party* was Tom's second successful role of 1984.

Hanks followed *Bachelor Party* with *The Man with One Red Shoe,* an Americanized version of a French film filled with comic intrigue. For his role as a professional musician, Tom even learned to play the violin. The movie was a flop,

---

Despite the success of Splash, *Tom's film career throughout much of the 1980s was a series of hits and misses. Although critics were kind about Tom's acting, such as his antic performance seen here in* Bachelor Party, *most of his films were flops at the box office.*

Tom mugs with Rita Wilson and John Candy in the comedy Volunteers. *During his ups and downs of the 1980s, the one bright light for Tom was his romance with Rita and their eventual marriage. It is reported that they have one of the happiest marriages in Hollywood.*

although several critics still found its star charming. At the same time he was suffering his first cinematic failure, Tom was also facing trouble at home. Samantha's career had not taken off as had Tom's, and their marriage was disintegrating.

Hanks did not dwell on negatives, however, and began filming another comic romp, *Volunteers.* Shot largely in Mexico, the film reunited Tom with John Candy and with Rita Wilson, who had guest starred on an episode of *Bosom Buddies* and was Tom's leading lady in *Volunteers.* Tom plays a spoiled rich guy who depends on his father to get him out of gambling debts and other messes. When the father refuses to fund his wayward son's misadventures, Tom's character joins the Peace Corps in Thailand. *Volunteers* also bombed. The star who had enjoyed two successive hits just one year earlier now had two blemishes on his box-office record.

Still, scripts continued to pour in, and Tom chose *The Money Pit*, a relatively big-budgeted comedy, as his next project. In the film, a young couple played by Tom and Shelley Long move into their dream home only to discover it's more of a nightmare than a dream as the house begins to collapse. Tom performed many of his own stunts in this film, including falling through a gaping hole in the floor while trapped in a rug and hanging from the second floor balcony when the staircase crumbles to dust beneath him.

Released in March 1986, the film received lukewarm reviews and a mixed reception at the box office. There was a positive result for Tom, however. He got a deal with Columbia Pictures for three films with the potential of $1 million per film. The first movie was a comedy-drama, *Nothing in Common,* and it would prove to be an important work in the career of the young actor. Although Tom played yet another successful, and likable, young man, the film explored many emotional issues that allowed Tom to show a side of himself that audiences had not yet seen.

The film tells the story of a young advertising executive, David Basner, whose mother decides to divorce her self-centered husband, Max. David is left trying to cope with an unbearable elderly man, played by Jackie Gleason, and their many generational differences. The film hit close to home for Tom, who had a sometimes problematic relationship with his own father.

"Some characters have nothing to do with you as a person; you create them from scratch. But occasionally, you have to draw from your own experience," he remembered. "That was the case here. I kept finding more of myself in this role. . . . David Basner even made me reconsider my own relationship with my parents."

Tom also had to consider other relationships as well. He and Samantha separated during the filming of *Nothing in Common* and would later divorce in 1987. During his separation Tom began dating Rita Wilson.

For Tom, this was a time of upheaval and bright spots. Here he was working with one of his childhood idols, Jackie Gleason. "The Great One," as Gleason was often called, was generous in his praise of Tom. "The verdict on Tom Hanks is that he's got it," he told a reporter. "Anybody can do a line, but Tom has moves. The right moves."

In *Nothing in Common*, Tom did have "it," at least as far as some critics were concerned. Although the movie was only a moderate financial success, they hailed Gleason's and Tom's performances as stellar. "Hanks does a masterly job . . . David is his richest, most revealing character yet," wrote *Time* magazine. "Never has Hanks or Gleason been better," raved *The Los Angeles Times*. And Leonard Maltin's *Movie & Video Guide* called Tom's performance "excellent." More importantly, Tom's acting in the film would prepare him for the more complicated roles he would take in the coming years.

Even before The *Money Pit* and *Nothing in Common* were released, Tom was back at work on the drama *Every Time We Say Goodbye*, set and filmed in Israel. He explained what attracted him to this story about a romance between an American pilot and an Orthodox Jewish woman from a strict family who fall in love during

World War II: "I was anxious to have the opportunity to work with a small group of people who do a special kind of story—out of the glare and attention. Working in an intimate, nonpressured way is something new for me. . . . I can concentrate on being an actor and not a movie star."

Tom thought that a dramatic project in a country far away from the intense media spotlight would enable him to continue stretching his acting muscles. Unfortunately, the film was a dismal failure, and never even appeared in theaters in Los Angeles.

Nineteen eighty-seven, however, brought the opportunity for Tom to prove himself again at the box office. The idea for a comedy film based on the 1950s and '60s TV police drama *Dragnet* was making the rounds in Hollywood and ended up with Dan Aykroyd and John Candy set to star. When Candy dropped out to participate in another project, Tom Hanks was offered the part of Aykroyd's partner, a sloppy detective with his own way of doing things.

After back-to-back dramatic roles, Tom was eager once again for the fun of a comedy. "Those two films [*Nothing in Common* and *Every Time We Say Goodbye*] required a lot of not just concentration but also emotional investment, which is very, very exhausting," he said. The comic mayhem and "cops and robbers" element of *Dragnet* was just what Tom needed to start his career on the upswing again. And working with someone like Dan Aykroyd, with whom he got along so well, made for a pleasant shoot. *Dragnet* became Hanks's first box-office hit since *Bachelor Party* three years earlier.

Tom's profile got a boost when he appeared as a co-presenter (with Bugs Bunny) at the Academy Awards ceremony in March 1987,

Tom was willing to take a supporting role opposite Dan Aykroyd (left) in the comic romp Dragnet. *The film was a chance to show his talent once again in comedy, making the movie one of Tom's hits of the 1980s.*

and his relationship with Rita Wilson was getting serious. On New Year's Eve 1987, Tom casually popped the question and they became engaged. They were married on April 30, 1988.

Tom's new marriage was only the beginning of his good fortune in 1988. Two high-profile projects were on his plate. First he took on *Punchline*, a poignant look at the lives of stand-up comedians. His costar, whom he called his "boss" because she had a producer credit on the film, was Sally Field, who became a friend to Tom and Rita during the shoot.

To research the characters' backgrounds, Tom made surprise stand-up appearances at comedy clubs in Los Angeles and New York City, and two real-life female comics advised

Sally. According to a New York gossip columnist, Tom's act, which consisted of funny observations about common, everyday situations went over with flying colors for a novice.

Tom had no idea what was in store for him next. He was to learn how it feels to be really big—both on screen and off. After filming *Punchline,* he took on a project that had been turned down by everyone from Harrison Ford to Robert De Niro. The film, called *Big,* is about a boy who makes a wish to be "big." He wakes up the next morning in an adult's body, but retaining a child's mind.

Big was a blockbuster. Much of the credit for the film's success went to Tom Hanks for his inspired performance as the not-so-grown-up Josh Baskin. Tom worked with the boy who played his character's "younger" self in order to mimic the young actor's mannerisms for a more realistic portrayal of a boy on the verge of puberty.

Audiences and critics together howled with laughter at Josh's antics. For the first time, "official" Hollywood noticed, too. Tom won the Golden Globe Award for Best Actor in a Comedy and was nominated for a Best Actor Academy Award. He did not win the Academy Award, but to be nominated for a comic performance, which is rarely done, showed that Hanks was indeed being taken seriously as an actor.

The accolades continued as Tom also earned the Los Angeles Film Critics Award for Best Actor for his roles in both *Punchline* and *Big.* Add to that the cover of *Newsweek* and his second gig hosting television's *Saturday Night Live.* It seemed as if the nation had come down with a serious case of "Tom Hanks Fever."

5

Tom Versus Career Disaster

With a new marriage, hit films, and his most successful year to date behind him, Tom Hanks carried on as he usually does—he continued to take on vastly different projects, but with mixed results. First up in 1989 was *The 'burbs*, a "sci-fi comedy." In the film, Tom leads his fellow suburbanites on a mission to discover the strange goings-on at an old, creepy house recently bought by some unusual new neighbors. *The 'burbs* opened well at the box office but then quickly disappeared from theaters because of poor audience reaction.

Turner & Hooch, Tom's next film, faired slightly better, though it did not capitalize on its star's growing dramatic talents. The plot was simple: Tom's cop character, Turner, partners with a dog named Hooch, who just happens to be the only witness to a grisly murder. The pair have to learn to cooperate with each other to solve the crime. *Turner & Hooch* received better overall reviews and became a financial success, earning about $70 million. Again, Tom Hanks was cited by critics for his fine performance, this time opposite a slobbering pooch.

Tom and Meg Ryan appeared together for the first time in the film Joe Versus the Volcano. *Despite Tom's popularity and success, he could not carry this film, and it appeared that his career was diving toward disaster.*

As the 1990s approached, Tom turned his attention to more original concepts in filmmaking and to roles that would challenge him. Unfortunately, "original" doesn't always mean "good" or "money-making." Hanks learned this lesson the hard way from his next two films, *Joe Versus the Volcano* and *The Bonfire of the Vanities*.

Joe Versus the Volcano was his first pairing with Meg Ryan. This film was not the hit that their subsequent films together would be, but it did show that the two had charisma as a screen pair. Although Tom's name above the title made it less of a failure than it would have been without him, the film was a disappointment.

Tom's second starring film in 1990, *The Bonfire of the Vanities*, was supposed to be the hit of the holiday film season for Warner Bros. Studios. Tom was paid a whopping $5 million for the central role of Wall Street wiz Sherman McCoy in the film based on the popular novel by Tom Wolfe. Sherman is not a typical Tom Hanks character. He is not a very nice man. The film revolves around the upheaval that occurs in Sherman's life after he and his mistress are involved in a headline-making scandal.

From the start, film critics and fans of the novel had their reservations about casting likeable Tom as the pompous and arrogant Sherman McCoy. Tom's character was not the only problem, however. Bruce Willis, who played a washed-up journalist, was an Australian in the book, and African-American actor Morgan Freeman was cast as a judge who in the novel is white and Jewish. Neither moviegoers nor critics accepted the satirical story, and the film died.

Fortunately for Tom, he emerged from the

disaster with little damage to his career or his appeal. After the film he took some time off to be with his family, during which time Rita gave birth to their first child, Chester. He also signed on with a new agency, Creative Artists, and sought a new direction for his career. As he later said: "I realized that it was more important to say no to stuff than it was to say yes. . . . My agent said, 'What do you want to do?' I said, 'Well, it's not like I know what I want to do, but I sure know what I don't want to do.'"

Tom eased back into films with an extremely low-profile role in the dramatic film *Radio Flyer* in 1992. In fact, at Tom's insistence, his performance and narration are not even listed in the film's credits. Continuing his "comeback,"

Teaming with Big's *director, Penny Marshall, Tom staged a stunning comeback as the hard-drinking, cranky, but lovable and caring baseball coach in* A League of Their Own. *Whether berating the opponents, squabbling with a call, or comforting a team member, he showed the versatility that has made him one of the film world's most sought-after actors.*

Teamed with Meg Ryan in their second film together, Sleepless in Seattle, *Tom portrayed the lonely widower with sensitivity and a touch of romanticism. Rita Wilson also had a part in the film.*

Hanks campaigned for a meaty supporting role in director Penny Marshall's next comedy. Marshall, who had directed Tom in *Big,* was reluctant at first to cast him as the drunken manager of an all-female baseball team during World War II. She changed her mind, but on one condition: Tom had to apologize in front of costars Geena Davis, Rosie O'Donnell, and Madonna for the last five movies he had made. He did.

In developing the poignant character of coach Jimmy Dugan, Tom gained 20 pounds. "I didn't want him to look like me," Tom said of the not-always pleasant Jimmy. "It was brand new turf for me. Because it wasn't the romantic lead of the movie. It was a big fat guy in the back, which actually was a blast to do. And it opened up a lot of avenues for me," Tom said.

The actor's habit of preparing for specific roles continued with *League*. Tom and the cast spent several months training on professional baseball fields. They bonded well together, with Tom often entertaining his colleagues with spontaneous puppet shows in the dugout during breaks in filming.

The film was a home run for Tom. It grossed more than $107 million and helped establish him as the most successful actor of his generation, besting such heavyweight competition as Arnold Schwarzenegger, Tom Cruise, and Harrison Ford. Tom Hanks was back.

In his first success of 1993, the sentimental romantic comedy *Sleepless in Seattle,* Tom acted opposite Meg Ryan for the second time. Released that summer, the film eventually sold $126 million in tickets and further solidified Tom's comeback. Making the film had not been a forgone conclusion, however. In fact, Tom had turned down the project after reading the original script. When director/co-writer Nora Ephron agreed to revise the script, he committed to the role of the lonely widower, Sam Baldwin, who finds love again with the help of his young son and a call-in radio show.

"We essentially rewrote every scene he was in. We would have these meetings where he was extremely cranky, and he would say, 'Well, this isn't what I would say in this scene,' and he would crankily explain what he might say. It was always funny and we'd type it up," Ephron later recounted.

The collaboration worked. The film, which pays homage to the 1957 tearjerker *An Affair to Remember* and featured many nostalgic love songs, has since become a romantic staple for couples everywhere. And in many articles about the film, Tom was compared again and again to legendary leading man James Stewart.

Tom did a serious about-face for his next role, taking on what some would say was the biggest risk of his career. As Andrew Beckett, the gay AIDS-infected lawyer fired from his prominent law firm, Tom took his dramatic skills to new heights in *Philadelphia.* The film was controversial from the start. First, its main character was a homosexual. Second, he had AIDS. Third, Tom Hanks was playing him. There were fears that "mainstream" audiences would not see the film and that the gay community would not accept Hanks in the role.

Those fears proved unfounded when the film premiered in December 1993. Some critics argued that Andrew's family was too supportive of his sexuality; others were concerned about the lack of love scenes between Andrew and his lover. Such criticisms were overshadowed by the powerful performances of Tom and his costars, who included Jason Robards, Mary Steenburgen, and Denzel Washington. Tom lost 30 pounds to realistically show the ravages of AIDS. The drama pleased enough people to make around $80 million, an astonishing amount for a film about the most dreaded illness of the last 20 years.

Talk of awards took on new significance when Hanks won a Golden Globe Award as Best Actor in a Drama in early 1994. And in March of that year, Tom took his first walk up the aisle of the Dorothy Chandler Pavilion to accept the Academy Award for Best Actor. The humbled and grateful actor gave a heartfelt

Tom was the first of Hollywood's leading men to portray a person with AIDS. In playing the dying gay lawyer in the film Philadelphia, *he took one of the biggest risks of his career. Taking the role only enhanced his image and also won him his first Academy Award for Best Actor.*

speech in which he thanked former teacher Rawley Farnsworth and a former classmate for their examples and defended the dignity of gay people and those suffering from AIDS. It was a truly unforgettable speech that brought tears to the eyes of many listeners.

Tom Hanks had won the highest award in film for a role that some said would ruin his career. The actor held up the gold Oscar statue, smiled, and said thank you. Ever the professional and gentleman, Tom's words said it all.

6

CULTURAL ICON

Beginning in 1993, Tom became interested in a different aspect of filmmaking: directing. When *A League of Their Own* became a TV series for a brief period that year, he was behind the camera for one episode. He followed that by directing an episode of Showtime's *Fallen Angels* and a segment from HBO's *Tales From the Crypt*. These experiences eventually led him to consider directing a feature film a couple of years later. First and foremost, though, he was an actor.

While still filming *Philadelphia,* Tom received a unique script about a slow-witted southerner who stumbles into some of the most important moments of the last 40 years, including teaching a young Elvis Presley to shake his hips and witnessing the Watergate break-in of the 1970s, all the while fighting for the woman he loves. A producer had been trying to get the story to the big screen for nine years without any luck. Then Tom Hanks expressed his interest.

The star was so impressed by the final version of the screenplay, titled *Forrest Gump,* that he immediately agreed to take the title role. Tom did not sign a standard contract,

---

The film world was doubtful about the outcome when Tom took on the role of the slow-witted Forrest Gump. The actor's gamble paid off, however. He won his second Academy Award and firmly established himself as an actor who could do no wrong.

however. Instead of a salary, he agreed to a percentage of the film's take. It was a gamble for a project that had been rejected so many times. But Hanks had faith in *Gump*, although he admitted he was "scared every minute" about capturing the larger-than-life character's nuances and his southern dialect.

The cast of the film included Robin Wright as Forrest's lifelong love, and Gary Sinise, who played the demanding role of Lieutenant Dan. Tom's younger brother, Jim, is also in the film, doubling for Tom in the scenes of Forrest's cross-country run. Although Sally Field is only a decade or so older than Hanks and had once played his potential love interest, she was offered the role of Forrest's mother. Field had been looking for the opportunity to reunite with Tom on screen, and she took the part.

"He's absolutely the most lovable human being on the planet. . . . Top-notch," said Field, explaining her decision to play Tom's mother. "First class in every category. . . . the familiarity and the love and all that was just there. Because we'd already worked together; because we were friends. It was just easy to be his mom."

And it was easy for audiences to fall in love with a Tom Hanks character all over again. The film opened in the summer of 1994 and topped the box office week after week, eventually taking in more than $330 million in ticket sales and becoming the number-one comedy of all time. It was also the fourth biggest moneymaker, behind *Star Wars*, *E.T.*, and *Jurassic Park*, until it was bumped to fifth in the wake of 1997's *Titanic*.

Talk of honors again swirled around Tom Hanks and the film. *Forrest Gump* merchandise flew off store shelves, and a restaurant bearing the character's name opened, with plans for more to come. Late night talk-show hosts and the general public quoted lines from the film such as "Life is like a box of chocolates . . . You never know what you're gonna' get" and "Run, Forrest, run!"

Tom and the film were showered with honors. "Hanks . . . can do no wrong as an actor," wrote a *Newsweek* critic. Toward the end of the year, Tom was recognized by the Hollywood Women's Press Club as being the person who "represents the best image of the entertainment industry to the world." They awarded him the prestigious Louella O. Parsons Award, bestowed in the past on such Hollywood royalty as Cary Grant and Bette Davis. *Entertainment Weekly* picked Hanks as Entertainer of the Year, and his immensely credible performance brought him another Golden Globe Award.

"Gumpmania" had some downsides as well. In addition to receiving more boxes of chocolates than he could ever possibly eat, Tom's privacy was increasingly being invaded. He spoke with *USA Weekend* about this loss of anonymity:

> I've been getting cuts in line at the airport for quite some time, so it has its advantages. . . . [But] some things I don't do anymore, like go to the bank, because it's too much trouble. I try to go to the same restaurants and stores, so they're used to me. Every once in a while, I'll go to a new one, and all hell breaks loose. Sometimes it's funny, and sometimes it's a hassle.

Forrest Gump received 13 Oscar nominations, including Best Picture and another Best Actor nod for Tom. The film ruled the Academy Awards ceremony in March 1995, winning

Best Picture and Best Actor, and earning further awards for director, screenplay adaptation, editing, and visual effects. As Tom stood before millions he heaped praise and thanks on his director, the cast, and his adoring wife. With this honor Tom became the first actor since Spencer Tracy to win back-to-back Best Actor awards.

History also figured prominently in Tom's next major role when he and old friend Ron Howard reunited for *Apollo 13.* This film may be closest to its star's heart. For some time, Hanks had wanted to bring the story of the ill-fated Apollo 13 space mission to the big screen. He knew it was the right time when Howard, who had the rights to the book *Lost Moon,* called and proposed the idea for the film.

Apollo 13 marked the first time Tom Hanks had portrayed a real-life person. He took the role of Jim Lovell, commander of the mission that had to return to earth without arriving on the moon when an unforeseen crisis occurred aboard the spacecraft. As he explained:

> This was a chance to play not just somebody that you admire greatly but somebody that I also think went through an almost superhuman experience and at the same time is made up of the flesh and blood you and I are. . . . I think this is kind of every little boy's dream come true . . . to play an astronaut.

So too did every able-bodied actor in Hollywood. Val Kilmer, John Travolta, and John Cusack pursued roles in the film, with parts eventually going to Kevin Bacon and Bill Paxton. Ed Harris, Kathleen Quinlan, and Gary Sinise rounded out the cast in strong supporting roles.

As a result, the film was more of an ensemble piece than some of Tom's recent projects. "Everybody has great moments in it, and everybody's really important to the core of the entire movie," said the modest Tom when questioned about the possibility of another Oscar nomination. "This is not one of those types of very flashy or attention-getting roles," he said.

Expectations were high for the film, but there was also concern. Not since the 1983 film *The Right Stuff*, which flopped with the public, had there been a historically accurate space movie. All fears vanished, however, as the space epic won ecstatic reviews and took in $25 million its

For Tom, portraying astronaut Jim Lovell in Apollo 13 was like a childhood dream come true. As a boy, he was obsessed with the space program, watching every mission and memorizing the names of the crews of the Apollo flights.

first weekend. *Apollo 13* was later nominated for several Academy Awards, including Best Picture, and was awarded Oscars for film editing and sound. A Tom Hanks film had scored again. For Tom personally, his per-film salary rose to $15 million.

In Tom's follow-up to *Apollo 13*, viewers would not find his image on film. But his distinctive voice and mannerisms were present. *Toy Story* was the first feature film to be entirely computer animated. Its director, John Lasseter, wanted well-known actors for the roles of the toys that come to life when Andy, the child who owns them, is not present. His first choice for Woody, a pull-string cowboy doll, was Tom Hanks. Lasseter has said that Tom "has the ability to take emotions and make them appealing."

The voice-over work on *Toy Story* began in 1993, after Tim Allen of TV's *Home Improvement* was hired to lend his voice for Buzz Lightyear, the astronaut action-figure who threatens to take Woody's place as Andy's favorite plaything. Working separately, Tom and Tim recorded dialogue every six months for two years. Tom has commented that the animated feature was one of the most daunting roles he has ever played. The hard work paid off, though. The film was a unanimous success—with critics, children, and adults alike. It earned a whopping $38 million its first weekend and eventually took in a staggering $192 million, again earning a Tom Hanks film a spot on the "biggest films in history" list.

With the successes of *Toy Story* and *Apollo 13* behind him, Tom and his "crack team of show-business experts" (as he calls his collaborators) set to work on a movie based on the

Tom was the voice of Woody the Cowboy in the animated film Toy Story. *He is well-known for taking roles not just for the salary he can command but for the enjoyment and satisfaction he gains.*

career of a fictional band that hits it big in the early 1960s. He chose this film, titled *That Thing You Do!*, as his directorial debut. He went even further by co-writing the script and many of the songs in the movie and taking a small role as the band's manager.

Tom picked his own cast, choosing mainly unknowns as the band, the Wonders. Amazingly, Tom Everett Scott, who played the band's drummer, bears a striking resemblance to the director. "Any kind of comparison to him is flattering. But I'm taller," Scott joked in an interview. *That Thing You Do!* was a modest hit upon release in the fall of 1996, after which Tom took a break from work to spend time with his family, including a new son, Truman, born in late 1995.

7

SECURE IN STARDOM

His stardom secure, Tom revisited his lifelong passion. Teaming once again with Ron Howard and Imagine Entertainment, he developed the miniseries *From the Earth to the Moon*, a 12-hour docudrama of the space program's Apollo missions. He wrote several of the critically lauded programs that aired on HBO in 1998 and directed the first episode, titled *Can We Do This?* Apparently, Tom could. "Visionary is not too strong a word for executive producer Tom Hanks's epic," wrote *TV Guide*, with *Variety* chiming in, "An extraordinary piece of filmmaking."

While Tom had kept busy with planning the miniseries and setting up his own production company, named Playtone, he had not appeared in a film for nearly two years. The project he chose for his return to the screen was *Saving Private Ryan*, the World War II story of a platoon's search for the sole surviving son of a military family. Teaming with producer-director Steven Spielberg, also a friend, they created an artistic and critical masterpiece that won five Academy Awards, including Best Director for Spielberg, as well as a financial success.

Tom talks with a crew member on the set of From the Earth to the Moon, *the Emmy-winning docudrama he cocreated, wrote, and produced. Although secure as a megastar who can afford to take time off, Tom continues to choose projects that challenge his acting, directing, and writing talents.*

The film's accolades were hard won and the roles demanding. Tom and his co-stars endured a six-day "boot camp" in an English forest to realistically portray men in combat. When the going got tough, the men took a vote on whether or not to continue the boot camp. Only one voted to stick it out—Tom. When they voted a second time, they all decided to continue.

"You can read books and see all the documentaries, but you're still not going to have a palpable understanding of how tired and cold and wet [the soldiers] are, and how heavy this equipment is, and how long it actually takes to walk three kilometers with all this stuff hanging from you," Tom told *Entertainment Weekly*.

Tom's colleagues had nothing but praise for their professional costar. "What Hanks does is lead by example. He could have ordered cracked crab from Alaska every day, because this business really does indulge people," actor Matt Damon commented. "But he didn't want the special treatment." Tom helped to develop the film's script and characters, meeting with Spielberg and the film's writer and producers. He even cut out a lengthy speech for his character, Captain John Miller, to help the characters and the film ring true. "It was a monologue any actor would kill to have, because my character finally got to drop this whole mantle. But I didn't want to drop the mantle. . . . It would just cheapen the character and compromise the integrity of who he is throughout the entire movie," he said about his emotionally guarded hero.

Reacting to a reporter's question regarding his children viewing the violent film, Tom said, "Not my kids, no. . . . [But] maybe it wouldn't be such a bad idea if a few young kids saw *Saving*

Private Ryan and came out of it weeping." Scores of adults experienced such a reaction, and the star himself admitted his strong feelings upon seeing the finished feature: "I didn't really know what I'd been involved in until Steven showed it to me. And I was emotionally crippled by it. I sat in the car for 20 minutes afterwards. I couldn't drive."

In fact, Tom and Spielberg were so affected by their film that they donated around $500,000 each to a D-Day Museum that is to open in New Orleans in the year 2000. And Tom, during his People's Choice Award acceptance speech for *Private Ryan*, also promoted the World War II memorial scheduled to be built in Washington, D.C. at the beginning of the 21st century.

Tom's next foray in front of the camera would not prove so emotionally taxing. Ever since *Sleepless in Seattle*, Tom had been asked if he would work with Meg Ryan again. Not until an update of an old classic, *The Shop Around the Corner*, came along did the time seem right. The older film also happened to be a Jimmy Stewart gem, which caused Tom some worry at first. As he explained: "But I decided to disregard that concern. . . . You'll never see me remake *Mr. Smith Goes to Washington* or *It's a Wonderful Life*. But [The] Shop Around the Corner is different. This is a very young Jimmy Stewart. This is Jimmy Stewart before Jimmy Stewart was Jimmy Stewart."

The updated movie, *You've Got Mail*, revolves around the relationship of two rival bookstore owners who anonymously fall for each other through E-mails. There is a problem, however. In their noncyber existence, the pair can't stand each other. In real life, the two stars have

Tom and Meg Ryan shared leading roles for the third time in the lighthearted comedy You've Got Mail. *Once again, critics gave Tom high marks for his comic instincts.*

no complaints about their relationship. "Every time we [make a movie], we pick up right where we left off," Tom explained. " Meg is very smart, and I always feel as though I have to be on my toes around her. . . . Meg makes me a better actor." Meg has responded by saying: "One of the things I just love about Tom is that he's incredibly democratic." She added that while filming in New York City, Tom was "waving at whole busloads of people as they drove by. It cracked him up, and it cracked them up."

What's next for Tom Hanks? In the summer of 1998 he filmed an adaptation of *The Green Mile*, a supernatural drama based on the serialized novel by Stephen King. The movie involves the relationship between a compassionate prison guard (Hanks) and an unusual prisoner (Michael Clarke Duncan) in the 1930s South. According to Tom, "You've never seen anything like this movie. It's like nothing else out there." Theater owners screening some of the film at the 1999 ShoWest Convention agreed, labeling the film a must see upon release at Christmas 1999.

While Tom has been creating dramatic waves, he is not neglecting his comic side. *Toy Story 2*, with Tom again voicing Woody, will be released in late 1999 and marks the first time the star has made a sequel. In January of 1999 he began filming *Cast Away*, a romantic comedy in which Tom is stranded on a desert island, separated for four years from his costar, Helen Hunt. Production on *Cast Away* was shut down for several months, however, so Tom was tentatively scheduled to do a "biopic" of singer Dean Martin in the interim.

Future projects include *Band of Brothers*, a World War II miniseries which Tom will executive produce for HBO, a live action and computer-generated version of the classic children's tale *Where the Wild Things Are*, and a new comedy for HBO.

Tom will continue his work for various charities, including the World War II Memorial, AIDS Project Los Angeles, and the I Am Your Child Foundation, a children's rights organization. He will also spend time with those he loves.

In between Tom's jobs, Rita works, and the

Tom could probably sign autographs day after day for his legions of fans. According to his friends, colleagues, and fellow actors, Tom's image as the "nice guy" is not a facade. His warmth, charm, and modesty are the real thing.

family travels together to film locations. "I have no best friend. The family is what takes up the vast amount of time," he told an interviewer in 1998.

It seems that Tom is the regular guy he has played all along. He is happy with it that way, and so are his fans. "I am always looking for something demanding. . . . But I'm never looking for change merely for the sake of change," he says of his "nice guy" roles. "I could play an evil guy tomorrow just for the sake of wanting to do it. But there would be no connection to the part."

Tom Hanks's modesty and his gratitude for his extraordinary success are genuine and endearing. He sums up his feelings this way: "I look at my own career and think, Hey, that's going pretty good. . . . I'd like to have a career . . . like I have!"

CHRONOLOGY

1956	Born Thomas J. Hanks on July 9 to Amos and Janet Hanks in Concord, California.
1961	Parents divorce; moves with his father, brother, and sister to Reno, Nevada.
1974	Graduates from Skyline High School; attends Chabot Junior College.
1976	Transfers to California State University at Sacramento.
1977	Interns at the Great Lakes Shakespeare Festival in Cleveland, Ohio; drops out of college.
1978	Moves to New York; marries Samantha Lewes; son Colin is born; joins the Riverside Shakespeare Company.
1980-82	Lands first film role in horror movie *He Knows You're Alone;* Shoots CBS TV movie *Mazes and Monsters;* stars in ABC sitcom *Bosom Buddies;* guest stars on *Taxi, Happy Days, Family Ties, The Love Boat,* and other TV shows.
1983	Films *Splash,* his first hit.
1984	Shoots *Bachelor Party.*
1985	Films *Volunteers* with leading actress Rita Wilson; stars in *The Money Pit.*
1987	Is divorced from Samantha Lewes; starts dating Rita Wilson.
1988	Marries Rita Wilson; films *Punchline;* stars in *Big* and wins a Golden Globe Award; nominated for Best Actor Academy Award.
1990	*Joe Versus the Volcano* and *The Bonfire of the Vanities* flop, prompting a 19-month break from acting; first child with Rita Wilson, Chester, is born.
1992	*A League of Their Own* is released, the first of his comeback films.
1993	*Sleepless in Seattle* is released; stars in *Philadelphia* and wins an Oscar; makes directorial debut with TV episodes of *A League of Their Own, Fallen Angels,* and *Tales from the Crypt.*
1994	Stars in *Forrest Gump.*
1995	Wins his second Oscar for *Forrest Gump;* son Truman is born.
1996	Directs first feature film, *That Thing You Do!*
1998	*From the Earth to the Moon* debuts on HBO; stars in *Saving Private Ryan,* which receives 11 Academy Award nominations; with Steven Spielberg donates funds to a New Orleans D-Day museum set to open in the year 2000.
1999	Films *Cast Away* with Helen Hunt; attends Academy Awards ceremony, appearing with astronaut and former senator John Glenn.

60

FILMOGRAPHY

1981	*He Knows You're Alone*
1982	*Mazes and Monsters* (made for TV)
1984	*Bachelor Party* *Splash*
1985	*The Man with One Red Shoe* *Volunteers*
1986	*Every Time We Say Goodbye* *The Money Pit* *Nothing in Common*
1987	*Dragnet*
1988	*Big* *Punchline*
1989	*The 'burbs* *Turner & Hooch*
1990	*Bonfire of the Vanities* *Joe Versus the Volcano*
1992	*A League of Their Own* *Radio Flyer* (uncredited performance/narration)
1993	*Philadelphia* *Sleepless in Seattle*
1994	*Forrest Gump*
1995	*Apollo 13* *The Celluloid Closet* (interviewee) *Toy Story* (voice only)
1996	*That Thing You Do!* (director, costar, and co-writer)
1998	*Saving Private Ryan* *You've Got Mail*
1999	*The Green Mile* *Toy Story 2* (voice only)
2000	*Cast Away*

SELECTED LIST OF HONORS

1978   Named Best Actor by the Cleveland Critics Circle for his role as Proteus in *The Two Gentleman of Verona*.

1988   Named Best Actor by the Los Angeles Film Critics Association for the films *Big* and *Punchline*.

1989   Receives Golden Globe Award for Best Actor in a Comedy for *Big*.

1994   Receives Golden Globe Award as Best Actor in a Motion Picture Drama for *Philadelphia*; receives Best Actor Academy Award for *Philadelphia*; receives Louella O. Parsons Award given by the Hollywood Women's Press Club; Named Entertainer of the Year by *Entertainment Weekly*.

1995   Receives Golden Globe Award as Best Actor in a Motion Picture Drama for *Forrest Gump*; receives Best Actor Academy Award for *Forrest Gump*; named Harvard University's Hasty Pudding Man of the Year; named ShoWest Box Office Star of the Year.

1998   Named one of the best actors of the 1990s and the 6th most powerful person in entertainment by *Entertainment Weekly*; receives the Hollywood honor of imprinting his hands in cement outside of Mann's Chinese Theatre.

1999   Receives People's Choice Award for Favorite Actor in a Drama for *Saving Private Ryan*; honored as ShoWest Box Office Star of the Decade.

FURTHER READING

Bart, Peter. *The Gross: The Hits, the Flops—the Summer That Ate Hollywood.* New York: St. Martin's Press, 1999.

Osborne, Robert. *70 Years of the Oscar: The Official History of the Academy Awards.* New York: Abbeville Press, 1999.

Pfeiffer, Lee, and Michael Lewis. *The Films of Tom Hanks.* Secaucus, NJ: Citadel Press, 1996.

Spielberg, Steven, and David James. *Saving Private Ryan: The Men, the Mission, the Movie—A Film by Steven Spielberg.* New York: Newmarket Press, 1998.

Trakin, Roy. *Tom Hanks: Journey to Stardom.* New York: St. Martin's Paperbacks, 1995.

ABOUT THE AUTHOR

JIM MCAVOY is a freelance writer and editor who lives and works in the Philadelphia area. This is his first book for Chelsea House. *Splash* and *Forrest Gump* have long been two of his favorite films.

ACKNOWLEDGMENTS

The author wishes to thank all those who helped in the research of this work, including Libby Wertin at the Center for Motion Picture Study-Margaret Herrick Library, John and Irene Brady, Megan McAvoy, and Don McAvoy.

PHOTO CREDITS:
Gregg De Guire/London Feature Int'l: 2; AP/Wide World Photos/Nick Ut: 6; 20th Century Fox/Photofest: 9, 25; AP/Wide world Photos/Dreamworks, David James, HO: 10; Photofest: 12, 28, 30; Columbia Pictures/Photofest: 15, 39; NOVA: 18; Paramount Pictures/Photofest: 20, 44; MCMLXXIII BUENA VISTA/Photofest: 26; Universal City Studios, Inc./Photofest: 34; Columbia TriStar/Photofest: 40; Warner Bros, Inc./Photofest: 36, 56; TriStar Pictures/Photofest: 43; AP/Wide World Photos/Universal Pictures/HO: 49; Walt Disney Pictures/Photofest: 51; Randy Tepper, HBO/AP/wide World Photos: 52; Nick Elgar/London Feature Int'l: 58.

INDEX